THE
B.O.S.S.
CAREGIVER

BALANCING LIFE, LOVE,
AND SELF-CARE WITH GRACE

By

L.P Golphin

I dedicate this book to my mother, who passed away in 2014. She was my biggest cheerleader, always believing in me and inspiring me to strive for my best. Mom, your love and encouragement continue to guide me, and this book is a testament to the lessons you instilled in me. You taught me the strength of compassion, the importance of resilience, and the power of hope. I pray this book reflects the values you hold dear.

TABLE OF CONTENTS

Welcome to Your
Journey as a B.O.S.S. Caregiver

"Caregiving is not just a responsibility; it's a journey of courage, love, and resilience. But even the strongest need tools to thrive."

Hello, wonderful caregiver. Welcome to a space created just for you. Let's be real, caregiving is not for the faint of heart. It is messy, unpredictable, and often feels like a whirlwind of tasks, emotions, and responsibilities. *The B.O.S.S. Caregiver* was created to equip you with the tools to lead with grace, to have the wisdom to balance your responsibilities, and to learn how to prioritize your own well-being.

This book goes beyond the traditional caregiving guide by focusing on practical strategies, emotional resilience, self-care, and empowerment. It introduces the unique B.O.S.S. mindset—**Balancing Obligations, Supporting, Self-care**—as a holistic framework to help you lead with strength while navigating the complexities of caregiving. Unlike books that focus solely on your loved one's needs, this guide places equal emphasis on *your* well-being, because the best care begins with a caregiver who feels supported and whole.

I want us to be upfront from the beginning—family caregiving isn't just demanding; it's one of the deepest acts of love and commitment you'll ever make. Some days, it's about managing daily tasks. Other days, it's about simply being the steady, reliable presence your loved one leans on. Whether you stepped into caregiving by choice or life handed it to you, the weight of responsibility is unquestionably real.

It is a lot! From juggling doctor's appointments and tracking medications to battling insurance red tape and making sure your loved one stays safe and well. This journey demands personal sacrifices and brings many unexpected twists and turns.

Inside these pages, you'll find open and honest discussion, practical strategies, and a whole lot of encouragement, all designed to help you to not just survive caregiving but *thrive* in it. We'll take a deep dive into what it really takes to balance your responsibilities, show up for your loved ones, and still make space for your own well-being. Because caregiving isn't just about managing tasks - it's about navigating the emotional, practical, and personal challenges with as much grace (and grit) as possible.

What is often not addressed is that beyond the day-to-day tasks, caregiving runs deep -it's emotional work too, not just practical activities. This element of caregiving is about learning to understand your feelings, process them in a healthy way, and ask for help without carrying guilt. It's about truly seeing your loved one's emotional world as well as your own and finding compassion for both of you along the way. Vulnerability isn't a weakness; it's where real strength begins.

My mission is to help you to both care for your loved one and ensure that you remember to care for yourself.

As a nurse and social worker, I have witnessed firsthand how caregiving stress can lead to serious health challenges. I have been that *listening ear* for countless caregivers whose anxiety and exhaustion have taken a toll on their physical and emotional well-being. That is why I cannot emphasize this enough: **self-care is not a luxury – it is essential.**

Early in my career, I assumed family caregivers would instinctively know how to manage the role or access resources. I thought, *"I gave them a list of what to do—they will figure it out".* But reality taught me otherwise. Caregiving is a massive undertaking, and most people are unprepared for the weight it carries.

Over time, I came to understand the physical, emotional, and spiritual toll caregiving takes. I have seen caregivers sacrifice their health, careers, and financial stability to fulfill their roles. I have heard stories of isolation, frustration, and heartbreak. These experiences strengthened my resolve to support caregivers in their responsibilities and help them to reclaim their joy, identity, and well-being. When caregivers thrive, so do the ones they care for.

For many, caregiving does not start with round-the-clock tasks. It begins with more minor but equally important acts of support. That was my experience. My mother was pretty independent, but over time, she needed more help with grocery shopping, rides to appointments, managing bills, and home repairs. At the same time, I was raising three kids, being a wife, and working full-time. It was overwhelming. My mother also struggled financially, and I often stepped in to help cover expenses. Watching her face those challenges was heartbreaking, especially knowing how hard she worked as a single parent, raising two children, and putting us through private school: sacrificing so much to give us better opportunities.

Like me, you may not even recognize yourself as a "caregiver" at first. The label does not always resonate. Many family caregivers quietly push through guilt, stress, and exhaustion - never naming what they are doing and never acknowledging what it is costing them. But that silence can lead to depression, anxiety, burnout, and strained relationships.

Caregiving is not just about completing a to-do list or making life easier for your loved one. It's about choosing to live *well* yourself. It's about making intentional choices that support your longevity, peace, and purpose—*because when you feel whole, you care from a place of grace, not depletion.*

What This Book Offers You

Caregiving is not a one-size-fits-all topic. Your journey is unique. Still, some threads connect all caregivers: the desire to give, the weight of responsibility, and the daily balancing act between caring for others and caring for yourself.

This book is here to walk alongside you with tools, hope, and a roadmap for success.

Here is what you will discover:

- **Strategies for Balance:** Learn how to set boundaries that protect your peace, delegate what you can, and manage your time so that caregiving does not take over your whole life.

- **Emotional Resilience:** Discover how to let go of guilt, make peace with imperfection, and stay connected to the deeper purpose that keeps you going, even on the hardest days.

- **Practical Tools:** Frameworks like C.A.R.E. and S.H.A.R.E. to simplify your responsibilities and help you build a strong, reliable support system.

- **Inspiration and Hope:** Quotes, stories, and reminders of your strength to keep you motivated, encouraged, and moving forward.

Why the B.O.S.S. Mindset?

The B.O.S.S. mindset—**Balancing Obligations, Supporting, Self-care**—is the heartbeat of this book. It is certainly not about expecting you to do more or be perfect. It's about helping you redefine success in caregiving—on *your* terms. It's about leading with grace, even on the hard days, and knowing that you are doing enough, even when it does not feel like it.

If you take away just one thing, let it be this: **You are not alone.** Together, we will navigate this journey with grace, resilience, and just the right amount of humor to keep it all in perspective. We will face the highs and lows, the wins and worries, side by side.

You've got this, and we have got each other.

C.A.R.E. in Action — Understanding the Framework of Family Caregiving

> "Caregiving: where hands that help are hearts that love, and every task is a testament to both."

Caregiving touches more lives than we realize—an estimated 53 million adults in the U.S. were unpaid caregivers in 2020 alone, according to the National Alliance for Caregiving and AARP. That is nearly **one in five** people stepping up to care for a loved one.

Let us pause for a moment and think about that.

Caregiving is not just a personal act of love and responsibility—it is an enormous, often invisible contribution to society. In fact, caregivers provide an astounding **$470 billion** worth of unpaid care each year, according to the AARP Public Policy Institute. Yes, you read that right— **a billion with a B**!

But here's the thing: this extraordinary labor of love often comes at a high personal cost—physically, emotionally, financially, and spiritually. These numbers don't just highlight how huge the caregiving world is, they show why it is vital to ensure caregivers have the resources, tools, and support they need to survive and **thrive**.

You are part of something highly significant, and your role matters more than you may realize.

The C.A.R.E. Framework: A New Way to Define the Role

Caregiving is a role that often sneaks up on us. It might start with running a quick errand, helping with groceries, or attending a doctor's appointment. Before long, those simple tasks evolve into something much more complex, and suddenly, you realize your life has shifted considerably.

I created the C.A.R.E. framework just for you to make this journey clearer (and a lot less overwhelming). The **C.A.R.E. Framework** stands for:

- **C**ompanion Assistance
- **A**ctive Support
- **R**egular Care
- **E**xtraordinary Care

This simple yet powerful model breaks caregiving into four stages, each with its own unique challenges and needs. By identifying where you are on this path, you can better understand your role, anticipate future demands, and seek the support that's currently right for you.

Let's break down each stage together.

Companion Assistance

Many caregivers begin here. At this stage, the role is about offering support that does not require a significant adjustment to one's life.

This is a lighter level of involvement—manageable alongside your day-to-day life. It might include:

- Driving a loved one to appointments
- Picking up groceries or medications
- Providing companionship
- Helping with minor household tasks

When my mother first needed help, I was in this stage. I ran errands, took her to the doctor, and helped around her house. It was all doable—until it wasn't. Juggling work, raising kids, and being a wife turned even these small tasks into a source of overwhelm.

Quick Tips for Companion Assistance:

- Use a shared digital calendar to coordinate errands and appointments
- Try grocery delivery apps to save time
- Be proactive and start building a support network before the need becomes urgent

Active Support

As caregiving evolves, so do the responsibilities. Active Support refers to providing regular help with daily living tasks and basic medical care. You might prepare meals, assist with bathing or dressing, manage medications, and monitor health conditions. This stage requires more time, energy, and organization.

As your loved one's needs increase, so does your role. Active Support includes:

- Assisting with meals, bathing, and dressing
- Managing medications
- Monitoring health conditions
- Coordinating routine medical care

I stepped into this stage when my mother had **bilateral knee surgery**. Suddenly, I was helping her with mobility, tracking appointments, and providing hands-on care. It was rewarding, but it stretched me in ways I had not anticipated.

Quick Tips for Active Support:

- Create a consistent daily routine to streamline care
- Keep a medication tracker or use an app for reminders
- Look into local services like meal delivery or adult daycare

Regular Care

Regular Care takes things up a notch. At this stage, caregiving becomes even more hands-on, with frequent support needed for chronic illnesses or disabilities. You might find yourself juggling multiple medical appointments, helping with mobility aids, and keeping track of complex medication schedules, all while pouring out a whole lot of time, energy, and heart.

The physical and emotional toll? It's very real, and it's very heavy.

At this level, caregiving becomes part of your everyday life. You might find yourself:

- Managing chronic health conditions
- Helping your loved one with mobility aids like walkers or wheelchairs
- Keeping track of complicated medication schedules
- Running to what feels like a never-ending stream of medical appointments

It requires constant coordination, and many caregivers explore **professional support** or respite services during this phase.

Quick Tips for Regular Care:

- Schedule respite care to protect your energy
- Use organizational tools like pill sorters or checklists
- Join a caregiver support group for emotional and practical guidance

Extraordinary Care

Extraordinary Care is where caregiving reaches a whole new level. Now, you're looking at full-time, high-need responsibilities that can feel overwhelming on every front. You might be providing constant supervision for a loved one with advanced dementia, handling complex medical tasks like wound care or tube feeding, and managing tough behavioral challenges. It's beyond exhausting—physically, emotionally, and mentally. Having professional help and building a strong support network isn't just helpful at this stage; it's essential.

This is the most intense stage of caregiving, where you may find yourself:

- Providing 24/7 supervision
- Handling advanced medical care (like wound care or tube feeding)
- Supporting loved ones through challenging behaviors caused by dementia or other serious health conditions

At this stage, professional assistance is **not optional but essential**. You will need a team, a plan, and a whole lot of grace.

Quick Tips for Extraordinary Care:

- Collaborate with healthcare providers to create a care plan
- Delegate tasks whenever possible—don't do it all alone
- Prioritize your mental health, even with small daily self-care breaks

Which Caregiver Are You?

So, where do you see yourself now?

- Are you the **Companion**, offering a helpful hand now and then?

- The **Active Supporter**, assisting with everyday needs?

- The **Regular Caregiver** navigating chronic care and complex routines?

- Or the **Extraordinary Caregiver**, carrying the full weight of high-level, daily support?

What's unique about caregiving is that it does not usually begin with a clear announcement. No one hands you a badge and says, *"Congratulations, you are a caregiver now!"* It often happens quietly and slowly, one responsibility at a time, until your whole life shifts before you know it.

That is why the **C.A.R.E. Framework** is so important. It gives you a name for where you are, a map to guide your next steps, and permission to ask for what you need.

Caregiving: A Journey of Love and Challenges

Caregiving is filled with beautiful, heart-opening moments. There is joy in connection, laughter, and deeply honoring someone you love. But let us not ignore the complex aspects:

- Watching someone you love decline

- Feeling isolated, even when people surround you

- Experiencing burnout

- Struggling with the financial, emotional, and physical weight it all brings

The emotional swings that result from these parts of caregiving can take a real toll. When caregivers neglect themselves, it often leads to **chronic health issues, emotional depletion,** and **a sense of being lost** in the process.

Let's change that narrative.

By embracing the C.A.R.E. Framework and being honest about your situation, you give yourself permission to seek help, set boundaries, and prioritize your well-being without guilt.

Caregiving is not just about showing up once; it is about staying strong enough to keep showing up day after day with love, compassion, and stamina.

> "Dispelling the myths of caregiving reveals the truth: it's not about being perfect, but about showing up with love, patience, and resilience each day."

Chapter 1 Takeaways

- **Be self-aware.** Many caregivers do not even realize they are caregivers until it affects their lives profoundly.

- **You need to know where you are *now*.** The C.A.R.E. Framework helps you define your role and your needs.

- **Every level has its challenges.** Whether Companion, Active Support, Regular Care, and Extraordinary Care.

- **Get the proper support and tools.** Recognizing your caregiving stage helps you access the resources you need.

- **Burnout is real.** But remember, it is also preventable.

- **Prioritize self-care.** Self-care is not selfish—it is survival.

- **Find power, peace and purpose.** Caregiving is both a challenge and an expression of love. Knowing your role more fully gives you these qualities.

Chapter 1 Reflection Questions

1. Which stage of the C.A.R.E. Framework best describes your
    current role?

    _____

    _____

    _____

    _____

    _____

    _____

2. What challenges are you facing, and what support might help
    you overcome them?

    _____

    _____

    _____

    _____

    _____

    _____

3. How can you prepare for the next stage of caregiving, if
    applicable?

    _____

    _____

    _____

    _____

    _____

Figuring out where you are in your caregiving journey can help you gain clarity about what you have to carry, where you need boundaries, and what support is available to you.

Caregiving isn't something you're supposed to do alone. There's real strength in reaching out and discovering true wisdom and self-awareness by using every tool that helps you grow and thrive.

You got this—and you are not alone.

Balancing Life and Caregiving — The B.O.S.S. Mindset

> "Balancing caregiving and life isn't about perfection; it's about creating a rhythm that honors both your loved one's needs and your own well-being."

Caregiving is often described as a balancing act, but let's be honest—it can feel more like juggling flaming swords while walking a tightrope! Finding time for yourself might seem impossible between work deadlines, family commitments, and caregiving responsibilities.

That is where the **B.O.S.S. mindset** comes in:

- **Balance obligations** without burning out

- **Support your loved one** with compassion and care while allowing others to support you

- **Self-care** is the foundation for your strength and resilience

Now, this is not just a catchy acronym—it is a roadmap, a strategy for managing caregiving without losing sight of your own well-being.

Let's not forget that caregiving is no small commitment—it is much more like taking on a part-time job. In fact, family caregivers dedicate an average of **23.7 hours per week** to caregiving tasks, according to the National Alliance for Caregiving. That is a large proportion of your day, every day of each week spent managing medications, scheduling appointments, and handling all the extras that come with supporting a loved one.

Now, throw in a full-time job, and it's no wonder so many caregivers feel like they are drowning. **Sixty-one percent** of caregivers are employed, and **60% of working caregivers** say they have had to cut back hours or take leave to manage their responsibilities. It is for this reason that tools, strategies, and support systems are not a luxury but a lifeline.

Let's walk through what this mindset looks like in action.

The Balancing Act

Balance does not mean splitting everything down the middle. In real life situations—some days, caregiving will demand more of your time. On other days, work or your personal life might need to take the front seat. Balance is about **flexibility** and giving yourself permission to adjust.

Think of caregiving as adding another "hat" to your collection—not replacing the others but learning how to wear them all without collapsing! One key strategy? **Time management.** Creating structure in your day can help you juggle caregiving, work, and rest.

Start with a weekly schedule. Plug in the non-negotiables first—appointments, work meetings, family events. Then, build caregiving tasks around those. And here's a biggie: **delegate**. You do not have to do it all. Let family, friends, or outside support help lighten the load.

Obligation Without Overload

The "O" in B.O.S.S. stands for **Obligation**—but that does not mean taking on *everything*.

Obligation is about knowing what **truly matters** and letting go of the rest. Not every task is urgent, and not every request deserves a "yes". Learning to **prioritize** and say "no" (without guilt!) is a game-changer.

Let's say your loved one needs someone to track their medications—that is a must. But baking cookies for the community fundraiser? That might be a "not right now" thing. Setting **boundaries** does not make you selfish—it makes you smart. And sustainable

Supporting Without Sinking

Caregiving is not a solo act. Even if you are the one in charge, **you don't have to do it alone.** The first "S" in B.O.S.S. stands for **Support**, as in support your loved one *and* allow others to support **you** while you do so.

So, who can you lean on? Maybe your sister can handle grocery runs. Perhaps your neighbor can sit with your loved one while you grab a break. Surely a friend can lend a listening ear when you just need to vent. But you need to ask, otherwise people may just not know you need help.

If your loved one is able, involve them in their own care. Let them have a say in meals, daily routines, or simple tasks. Empowering them gives them dignity and gives you breathing space.

Practical Tips for Supporting:

- **Build a support network**: Reach out to family, friends, and community resources.

- **Use technology**: Shared calendars and caregiving apps can simplify coordination.

- **Communicate openly**: Have honest conversations about what your loved one needs and how others can assist.

The Power of Self-Care

Now let's talk about the second "S"—**Self-care**. And I know, I know… when you are already stretched thin, the last thing on your list is a bubble bath.

But here is the truth: **You cannot pour from an empty cup.**

Self-care does not have to mean a spa day. It can be a quiet cup of tea, a walk around the block, a five-minute breathing break, or laughing at a funny meme. It is the small moments that restore you. And the basics matter too—**sleep, hydration, nutrition**—they are your fuel.

Mindfulness practices like meditation or journaling can also help center you. And most importantly, do not underestimate the healing power of laughter. Joy is medicine.

Practical Tips for Self-Care:

- **Schedule it**: Put it on your calendar—seriously.

- **Start small**: 5 to 10 minutes of quiet can shift your energy.

- **Seek support**: Therapy, coaching, or support groups are valid and valuable.

When Life Gets Overwhelming

Even with all these tools, the indisputable fact is—there will be days when caregiving feels like **too much**. That's normal.

Decision fatigue, guilt, frustration—it all piles up. The trick is recognizing it and taking action before you burn out.

When you feel those indicators of approaching burnout creeping in, take a breath, ask for help, and tap into respite care services. Even one day off can give you the clarity and strength to keep going.

The B.O.S.S. Mindset in Action

Let me share a little of my story.

When my mother had bilateral knee surgery, my caregiving role quickly shifted from light support to full-on **Active Support**. I managed her recovery, coordinating physical therapy, cooking, cleaning—you name it. It was *a lot*.

But I paused. I leaned into the B.O.S.S. mindset. I focused on what mattered most—her healing. I created a weekly plan, protected time for my kids and work, and ensured I did not let go of my self-care.

I also **reached out for help**. I did not try to do it all.

That's what being a B.O.S.S. caregiver is all about—it not about doing everything perfectly. It is about **prioritizing, protecting your peace, and allowing support in.**

So, let me ask you: How can you embody the B.O.S.S. mindset today?

"Caregiving isn't about doing it all—it's about doing what matters most, seeking support when needed, and finding grace in the balance between care and self-care."

Chapter 2 Takeaways

- **Balance is flexible.** It is not about doing everything evenly, but adjusting priorities as needed.

- **Not all obligations are equal.** Say yes to what matters and no to what doesn't.

- **Support systems matter.** You do not have to do this alone—lean on your network.

- **Self-care is essential.** Even small habits help you stay strong and sane.

- **Burnout can be prevented.** Recognize the signs and take action early.

- **Decision fatigue is real.** Step back when needed, delegate, and use available resources.

- **Progress, not perfection.** You are doing enough. Celebrate the small wins.

- **You are not alone.** The B.O.S.S. mindset gives you the clarity and confidence to thrive.

Chapter 2 Reflection Questions

1. What does "balancing obligations, supporting others, and self-care" mean to you personally?

    _____

    _____

    _____

    _____

    _____

2. Which part of the B.O.S.S. mindset feels most challenging for you right now? Why?

    _____

    _____

    _____

    _____

    _____

3. How can you apply the B.O.S.S. mindset to your caregiving journey this week?

    _____

    _____

    _____

    _____

    _____

You are on your way to becoming a B.O.S.S caregiver. Your journey begins here.

Finding Balance in the Chaos — Navigating Stress, Guilt, and Burnout

" Caregiving is not about perfection, it's about resilience, recognizing when you're stretched too thin, and finding the courage to ask for help."

Caregiving is no small task. We have to be real here—it can push even the strongest among us to the edge. Studies show that **40–70% of caregivers experience symptoms of depression** that go far beyond just "feeling down" (Family Caregiver Alliance, 2021). That is a massive emotional toll. And it does not stop there—**23% of caregivers report that their health has suffered** due to the constant demands of caregiving (National Alliance for Caregiving, 2020).

These numbers are more than statistics—they're a wake-up call. They remind us that if we do not take care of ourselves, we risk burnout, exhaustion, and serious health issues. As much as caregiving is an act of love, it can also become a source of depletion if we are not careful. And if your own health is suffering, how on earth will you care for yourself, let alone someone else?

Let's face it: caregiving is an emotional and physical rollercoaster that rarely slows down. Sure, there are many gratifying moments, but there are also days that leave you drained, frustrated, and wondering if you are doing enough. The truth is that **stress, guilt, and burnout** are just as real as the to-do list. The key is learning how to recognize, prevent, and manage these challenges before they take over.

That's where the **S.O.S. mindset** comes in:

- Stressed
- Overwhelmed
- Support Needed

Think of it as your internal alarm system. When you feel that tension building, S.O.S. is your cue to pause, reflect, and take intentional steps toward balance. Let's explore how.

Recognizing the Signs of Stress

Caregiving often starts small—running errands, attending appointments, helping with the basics. But it can quickly evolve into something much bigger, with more demands than you expected. Before you know it, you are stretched thin, running on fumes, and feeling like there is no space left to breathe.

Common signs of caregiver stress:

- Feeling irritable or impatient, even over small things

- Constant worry about your loved one's care, even when things seem okay

- Neglecting your own basic needs—skipping meals, losing sleep

- A lingering sense of guilt that no matter what you do, it is not enough

Quick Tips for Managing Stress:

- **The 4-7-8 Breathing Technique**: Inhale for 4 seconds, hold for 7, exhale for 8

- **Movement Breaks**: A quick stretch or walk can reset your mind

- **Mindful Moments**: Set a 2-minute timer, close your eyes, and just *breathe*—no screens, no to-do list

Stress is normal, but it is also a warning signal, and it is crucial that you listen to it and take action. Ignoring it will not make it go away—it will continue to grow louder until it affects your health, relationships, and ability to care.

The Weight of Guilt and Overwhelm

Guilt is a sneaky companion in the caregiving journey. You might feel guilty for not doing enough. Guilty for needing a break. Guilty for feeling frustrated. Guilty for... breathing?!

Let's pause right here: **Guilt is a liar.**

It tells you that you are failing when you are actually showing up, day after day, doing your absolute best.

Reframing Guilt:

- **Acknowledge your efforts**: Write down three things you are doing well as a caregiver.

- **Flip the script**: Would you tell a friend in your shoes that they are not doing enough? No? Then extend that same grace to yourself.

- **Set boundaries without apology**: Saying "no" to what drains you is saying "yes" to your wellness.

Then there is **overwhelm**—the weight of everything you are carrying—all the lists, tasks, appointments, and emotions. It is the feeling that even one more request might break you.

Ways to Combat Overwhelm:

- **Break it down**: Don't focus on the big picture. Just take the next step.

- **Delegate**: Let someone else take care of something—anything.

- **Reframe the narrative**: Instead of "I have too much to do," try "I will do one thing at a time".

Practical Strategies for Managing Stress and Guilt

The first step? Acknowledge how you feel. No shame. No guilt. You are human. Caregiving is demanding physically, emotionally, and mentally.

Permit yourself to feel stressed without judgment. *Please remember that: You are human, after all.*

Strategies to Regain Your Balance:

- **Micro-breaks**: Step outside. Breathe. Listen to a song that lifts your spirits.

- **Delegate tasks**: Grocery delivery? Cleaning help? Take it.

- **Set boundaries**: If it is too much, say no. You do not owe anyone an explanation.

- **Journal it out**: Writing can help release tension and bring clarity.

- **Use the S.O.S. signal**: When it feels like too much, *speak up. Reach out.* You do not have to do this alone.

The Role of Support

Caregiving can feel isolating, but it doesn't have to be a solo mission. Many caregivers wait too long to ask for help, often out of guilt, pride, or fear of being a burden. But **building a support network** is one of the most powerful tools in your toolkit.

Ways to Build Support:

- **Family & friends**: Be specific when asking for help. "Can you bring a meal?" is clearer than "I need help".

- **Professional services**: From home health aides to therapy, there is no shame in leaning on professionals. That's what they are there for.

- **Technology**: Use caregiving apps, group texts, or shared calendars to delegate and update without added stress.

Avoiding Burnout

Burnout is not just about being tired, it's a **state of emotional, mental, and physical depletion** in which one feels like there is nothing left to give.

The best way to avoid burnout? **Make self-care non-negotiable.**

Self-Care Tips to Prevent Burnout:

- Stick to a sleep schedule—even if you need help to get uninterrupted rest.

- Protect time for something that brings you joy, even if just 15 minutes daily.

- Practice mindfulness to ground yourself in the present.

- Know when to take a break—yes, stepping away is okay.

> "Caring for someone else is an act of love; caring for yourself is how you keep that love alive."

Chapter 3 Takeaways

- **Stress is normal, but it is also manageable.** Learn the signs and take action early.

- **Guilt does not define you.** It shows you care, but it should not control your actions.

- **Overwhelm is a signal.** Recognizing S.O.S signals helps you pause and realign.

- **Breaks are vital.** Even small moments of rest can refresh your energy.

- **Support matters.** You are not meant to do this alone—build your community.

- **Burnout is preventable.** Make self-care a priority, not an afterthought.

- **You are not alone.** Asking for help is an act of strength and love.

Chapter 3 Reflection Questions

1. What caregiving responsibilities feel the most overwhelming, and how are they affecting your well-being?

   _____

   _____

   _____

   _____

   _____

   _____

2. Have you noticed any changes in your physical, mental, or emotional health since becoming a caregiver? What steps can you take to prioritize your health?

   _____

   _____

   _____

   _____

   _____

3. What small, manageable way can you care for yourself this week?

   _____

   _____

   _____

   _____

   _____

You do not have to be perfect to be a phenomenal caregiver. You just need to stay connected to yourself, your limits, and the people who can support you.

Asking for help does not make you weak. It makes you wise.

Building Bridges — Creating a Support Circle with the S.H.A.R.E. Framework

"Caregiving isn't meant to be a solo act. True strength comes from knowing when to share the weight."

Let me tell you something you may not have even thought of—**caregiving is not a solo mission.** It can feel like it, especially when you are the one juggling meds, meals, and mood swings. Research backs up what many caregivers already know in their hearts: **support matters.**

Studies show that caregivers with a strong support network experience **22% lower levels of stress and depression** (American Psychological Association, 2020). **64% of caregivers** already rely on family members for some level of help (AARP, 2020). That means if you are carrying everything on your own, it is time to loosen your grip and invite others in.

Because caregiving is not just about giving—it's about **connecting, collaborating,** and **sharing** the responsibility. You deserve that kind of care, too.

Why You Need a Support Circle

Let's cut to the chase: caregiving can feel like it consumes your whole life. Rest? Reflection? Relief? Often in short supply. But here is the truth—**no one is meant to carry this alone**. It may not feel easy to reach out, but building a **reliable support circle** is more than helpful—it is essential.

A sound support system keeps you from burning out, provides backup when life throws a curveball, and ensures your loved one is well cared for even when you are not at 100%.

To make support practical (not just theoretical), I created the **S.H.A.R.E. Framework**:

- Simplify
- Handoff
- Allow
- Review
- Express

Let's walk through how each step helps build bridges and break down barriers.

S is for Simplify

Caregiving comes with a *mile-long* to-do list: doctor's appointments, medications, meals, laundry, emotional support—you name it. Simplifying does not mean slacking off. It means focusing on what truly matters and finding **innovative, efficient ways** to handle everything.

Think of this as *decluttering your caregiving role.* When you simplify, you free up mental and emotional energy, so you have the bandwidth to respond when those inevitable emergencies pop up.

Quick Tips for Simplifying:

- **Use technology**: Set reminders for meds. Try apps for scheduling or caregiving checklists.

- **Batch tasks**: Group similar errands together to save time and energy.

- **Invest in time-savers**: Meal kits, grocery delivery, or recurring/delivered prescriptions can simplify daily demands.

- **Prioritize using the K.I.S.S. method (Keep it Sweet and Simple): Focus on the essentials** and let the rest go.

H is for Handoff

You do **not** have to do everything yourself. Trying to be Superwoman will only lead to burnout.

Handoff is all about delegation. Think of it as caregiving teamwork. Identify tasks others can help with and be specific when you ask them.

Instead of "I need help," try:

"Can you take Dad to physical therapy on Thursdays?"

"Would you be able to handle grocery shopping this week?"

Ways to Effectively Delegate:

- **Family Involvement**: A sibling could manage finances or handle medical paperwork.

- **Community Support**: Ask church members, neighbors, or local organizations for assistance.

- **Professional Services**: Hire a cleaning service or home health aide for routine support.

- **Be direct**: The clearer you frame your questions, the more likely you will get a "yes".

Delegating is not weakness—it's wisdom.

A is for Allow

This one? It's tough. Allowing others to step in takes trust—and sometimes letting go of perfection.

We often think, *"No one can do it like I can"*. But guess what? That mindset isolates you. When you **allow** others to help, you give your loved one access to different kinds of support while giving yourself space to breathe.

Ways to Practice Allowing:

- Let your teenager handle grocery shopping—even if they buy the "wrong" brand!

- Accept your neighbor's offer to sit with your loved one while you run errands.

- Let your loved one help with small tasks (if able), like folding laundry or picking up meals.

Mindset Shifts for Allowing:

- Receiving help is a strength, not a failure.

- Others may do it differently, and that is okay.

- Rest is essential to showing up with compassion, not resentment.

R is for Review

Once you have simplified, handed off tasks, and allowed others to support you, remember to **review** how it is going.

This is not about micromanaging. It is about **communication** and **course-correction.**

Check in with your circle. See what is working and what is not. If someone is struggling to keep up, be flexible and reassess.

How to Review Effectively:

- **Check in regularly**: "Hey, how is the meal plan working out? Need any help?"

- **Reevaluate as needs change**: Adjust responsibilities if your loved one's health shifts.

- **Be adaptable**: People's capacity to help can change—stay flexible and update the plan.

Reviewing keeps everyone on the same page and ensures the care flows smoothly.

E is for Express

Last but never least—**express your feelings**.

Whether communicating gratitude, stress, appreciation, or even frustration, expressing your emotions strengthens relationships and helps others feel seen and valued.

Caregiving can get heavy. Do not hold it all in. A heartfelt thank-you, a check-in text, or a shared laugh can go a long way.

Ways to Express Gratitude & Emotions:

- Say "thank you" often and sincerely.

- Write a short note or offer a small gift of appreciation.

- Share your feelings in a safe space—vent to a trusted friend or join a support group.

- Celebrate wins, big or small, together.

> " Strength isn't about doing it all; it's about knowing when to share the load and trusting others to help you carry it."

Chapter 4 Takeaways

- **Simplify:** Streamline your caregiving tasks to reduce overwhelm.

- **Handoff:** Delegate clearly to family, friends, or professionals.

- **Allow:** Trust others to help, even if it means letting go of "your way".

- **Review:** Check in regularly to adjust responsibilities and ensure everyone feels supported.

- **Express:** Say thank you, celebrate wins, and share your feelings freely.

The **S.H.A.R.E.** framework helps you turn caregiving from carrying the weight alone to building a real support system you can count on. When you build those bridges, you're not just getting help but strengthening your village and making the journey a little lighter.

Chapter 4 Reflection Questions

1. Who is currently in your support circle, and how do they contribute?

   _____

   _____

   _____

   _____

   _____

2. What tasks or responsibilities could you delegate to lighten your caregiving load?

   _____

   _____

   _____

   _____

   _____

3. How can you strengthen communication with your support network to build trust and collaboration?

   _____

   _____

   _____

   _____

   _____

Support is out there—but sometimes, you have to give yourself permission to receive it.

You are not meant to carry this all alone.

Pause for Peace — Setting Boundaries that Protect and Empower

"Boundaries are not walls to keep others out; they are bridges that protect your well-being while allowing meaningful connections to flourish."

Caregiving is a labor of love but one that can become all-consuming without clear boundaries. Many caregivers are torn between their responsibilities and the life they once knew. Saying "yes" too often might feel loving, but it often leads to burnout, resentment, and strained relationships.

The truth is that setting boundaries is not about pushing people away. It is about protecting your peace, preserving your health, and making space for what matters most. In fact, caregivers who set healthy boundaries report **30% fewer symptoms of stress and burnout** (Journal of Applied Gerontology, 2019). When you delegate effectively, you free up time and reclaim energy. According to the National Institute on Aging, delegation can **improve your time efficiency by 15–20%**.

This is where **the P.A.U.S.E. Method** comes in—a practical, compassionate approach to setting boundaries that serve both you and your loved ones.

The P.A.U.S.E. Method:

- Pause and Reflect

- **A**ssert Needs

- **U**nderstand Pushback

- **S**tay Consistent

- Evaluate and Adjust

Let's walk through each step together.

P – Pause and Reflect

Caregiving can feel like a never-ending whirlwind. You are doing so much that your own needs get pushed aside. But without **pausing**, it is hard to notice when your limits are being crossed, before it goes too far.

Reflection helps you identify what is draining you, what is working, and where boundaries are needed. It is not just about what is going wrong, but about reconnecting with yourself.

Practical Reflection Steps:

- **Create quiet moments**: Journal, meditate, or take a mindful walk.

- **Ask key questions:**

    - What caregiving tasks feel most overwhelming?

- How is this affecting my health and happiness?

- Where do I feel overextended or resentful?

• **Spot the energy drainers**: Notice which tasks, situations, or people leave you depleted.

• **Celebrate wins**: Reflection also means recognizing what you are doing well.

Caregiving Scenario: Amber's Reflection

Amber, a midlife caregiver for her father, realized she was running on fumes when she broke down in tears over a simple scheduling conflict. During her reflection time, she identified that:

• She was tired of being the sole decision-maker.

• Weekly transport was exhausting.

• She had zero time for herself.

So, she asked her brother to handle appointments and blocked Sunday afternoons for self-care.

Tools for Reflection:

• **Wheel of Life Assessment:** Create a circle divided into key areas of your life (e.g., caregiving, work, relationships, health, hobbies). Rate your satisfaction in each area on a scale of 1–10. This visual can highlight where boundaries might help.

- **Stress Inventory:** Write down your daily caregiving tasks and rate them from 1 (least stressful) to 5 (most stressful). Look for patterns and prioritize where change is needed.

- **Gratitude Focus:** End each reflection session by listing three things you are grateful for. This shifts your mindset from problem-focused to solution-oriented.

The Power of Reflection

Pausing to reflect is not just some nice little activity—it is highly necessary. It helps you reconnect with your sense of purpose as a caregiver while ensuring you do not lose yourself in the process. Reflection clarifies what is truly important, enabling you to create boundaries that protect your time, energy, and emotional well-being.

Action Step:

Schedule a weekly 15-minute reflection session. This is where boundaries begin—with awareness.

A – Assert Needs

Let's clarify something: asserting needs does not mean being harsh or inflexible. It means communicating **clearly and kindly**.

You cannot expect others to meet your needs, if you never tell them about them.

Why Asserting Needs Matters

Caregivers often fall into the trap of assuming that others should automatically know what they need. This leads to unmet expectations, frustration, and even resentment. Clearly articulating your needs sets the stage for healthier communication and more effective support.

How to Assert Your Needs:

- Be **specific**: "Can you take Mom to therapy on Wednesdays?"

- Use **"I" statements**: "I need time to rest on Saturdays. Can you handle meal prep then?"

- **Stay respectful**: Use a calm tone and open body language. Keep it a conversation, not a confrontation.

Caregiving Scenario: Bonita Speaks Up!

Bonita, overwhelmed by her caregiving responsibilities, realized she needed help managing her mom's medications. Instead of assuming her sibling would not help, she said, "I have been handling all of Mom's medication refills, and it's becoming too much for me. Can you take over this responsibility starting next week?"

Action Step:

Write down one task you would like to delegate. Practice asking for help clearly and respectfully.

U – Understand Pushback

Not everyone will cheer for your new boundaries. Some might resist, especially if they are used to you doing *everything*.

Pushback does not mean you are wrong. It means change is hard. Stand your ground with **grace and confidence**.

Why Pushback Happens

Pushback often stems from others feeling inconvenienced or resistant to change. Some may have become used to relying on you for everything, while others may not fully understand your limitations.

How to Handle Pushback:

- Stay **calm**: Do not match their frustration.

- **Reiterate your need**: "I know this is new, but I need to make this change to stay well."

- **Show empathy**: "I get that this might feel inconvenient, but I hope we can work together."

Caregiving Scenario: Emily's Experience

When Emily told her brother she could not attend every appointment anymore, he said, "But you've always done it". She replied, "I am stretched too thin and need us to share this. Let's make a plan together".

Action Step:

Think of a time someone resisted your boundary. Now, plan how to respond calmly, empathetically, and clearly next time.

S – Stay Consistent

It is one thing to set a boundary—it is another to stick with it. If you have too many exceptions, people will stop taking them seriously.

Consistency sends the message: *"I mean this."*

Why Consistency Matters

Inconsistency sends mixed messages and can undermine your efforts to establish boundaries. By staying consistent, you reinforce the importance of your needs and demonstrate commitment to self-care.

Staying Consistent Tips:

- **Set expectations early**: Make the boundary known and understood.

- **Follow through**: Even if it is hard, hold the line.

- **Use gentle reminders**: "Remember, I can only talk about caregiving after work hours."

Caregiving Scenario: Eva's Consistency

Eva had set a boundary about work-hour interruptions, but her brother continued to call. Instead of ignoring it, Eva gently reminded him: "I really need us to stick to discussing caregiving tasks after 6 p.m. It helps me stay focused during the day."

Action Step:

Choose one boundary you have struggled with. Write out how you will reinforce it moving forward.

E – Evaluate and Adjust

Boundaries are not one-size-fits-all or set-it-and-forget-it. Life changes, health changes, and needs change, so your boundaries should, too.

Why Evaluation is Important

Caregiving responsibilities and circumstances change over time. What worked six months ago might not be effective today. Regularly reassessing your boundaries ensures they remain relevant and helpful.

When and How to Adjust:

- **Set regular check-ins:** Monthly or quarterly, ask yourself, "Is this still working?"
- **Get feedback:** Ask trusted family members how the boundary is affecting them.
- **Adjust with intention:** If your loved one's needs increase, rebalance your commitments.

Caregiving Scenario: Yolanda's Adjustment

When Yolanda's mom's care needs increased, Yolanda added a shared family calendar and reassigned tasks among her siblings. The boundary shifted, but her self-care stayed protected.

Action Step:

Review your current boundaries. Which one needs adjusting? Plan the next step.

> "Setting boundaries is not selfish, it's a form of self-respect that empowers you to care with strength and purpose."

Chapter 5 Takeaways

- **Pause and Reflect:** Awareness is the first step toward healthy boundaries.

- **Assert Needs:** Speak clearly, kindly, and specifically.

- **Understand Pushback:** Expect it, but do not let it derail you.

- **Stay Consistent:** Boundaries only work when you honor them.

- **Evaluate and Adjust:** Boundaries should evolve with your caregiving journey.

Boundaries are not barriers—they are bridges. They help you care with intention instead of obligation. They protect your peace, and they remind you: you matter too.

Chapter 5 Reflection Questions

1. What boundaries do you currently have in place, and how effective are they?

_____

_____

_____

_____

_____

_____

2. What is one caregiving area where you need to set more precise limits?

_____

_____

_____

_____

_____

_____

3. How can you stay consistent, even when others resist your boundaries?

_____

_____

_____

_____

_____

_____

Remember: creating boundaries is not about backing away from love—it is about showing up fully present because you have protected your energy first.

You are not just a caregiver. You are a B.O.S.S. caregiver, and boundaries are one of your most powerful tools.

Let the Light In —
Embracing the L.I.G.H.T. Framework

"In the shadows of caregiving, even the smallest glimmers of light can guide you toward hope and renewal."

Caregiving can sometimes feel like walking through a dark tunnel with no clear end. The emotional, physical, and mental demands can feel relentless. But even in the darkest moments, there are small rays of light—beautiful glimmers of grace, gratitude, and growth.

Here is a little-known secret—gratitude and self-care are secret weapons. Practicing gratitude can reduce symptoms of depression and anxiety, and simple mindfulness habits like deep breathing or guided meditation can help regulate emotions and bring you back to center.

These are not grand solutions. They are small but mighty tools that, when practiced consistently, can bring you peace, perspective, and a renewed sense of purpose.

That is where the **L.I.G.H.T. Framework** comes in—a gentle, practical guide to help you reconnect with joy and resilience through five powerful principles:

- Look for Small Wins

- Incorporate Self-Care

- Gratitude is key

- Honor Your Feelings

- Think Positively

Let's explore how to let more light in—one breath, one boundary, and one blessing at a time.

L — Look for Small Wins

Caregiving can feel like a marathon, and it's easy to focus on everything that's not going right. But there is power in pausing to notice the little victories that often go unseen.

Why Small Wins Matter:

When you focus on small successes, you shift from surviving to thriving. It helps you recognize that your efforts are making a difference, even if the progress feels slow.

Ways to Celebrate Small Wins:

- **Set realistic goals:** Break larger tasks into smaller, achievable steps.

- **Create a "win" journal:** Write down something you did well each day.

- **Acknowledge effort:** Progress is not always perfect, but effort matters.

Caregiving Scenario: Robert's Wins

Robert, who cares for his father with Alzheimer's, began celebrating moments like getting him to take medication without resistance or sharing a laugh at breakfast. These small joys helped him stay grounded and positive.

Action Step:

Write down one big or small win at the end of each day. Let it be a reminder that you're making a difference.

I — Incorporate Self-Care

Let's be honest: "self-care" often sounds like a luxury concept that caregivers cannot afford. But real self-care is not about spa days or long vacations but small, consistent acts that restore your energy.

Self-Care in Action:

- **Time-block micro-breaks:** Even five minutes to stretch, breathe, or sip tea counts.

- **Anchor moments:** Practice mindfulness while folding laundry or making tea.

- **Quick rituals:** Light a candle, play your favorite music, or apply your favorite lotion.

Caregiving Scenario: Eric's Routine

Eric, a father of two and caregiver for his mother, began taking a 10-minute walk after dinner. That small break became his daily reset, helping him face each evening with calm and clarity.

Action Step:

Choose one self-care habit that fits your current routine and commit to doing it daily for one week. Small actions lead to big shifts.

G — Gratitude is Key

Gratitude is like turning on a light in a dark room. It does not remove the chaos, but it will help you see the good that still exists.

Ways to Practice Gratitude:

- **Gratitude journal**: List three things you are thankful for each day.

- **Ritualize it**: Share a moment of gratitude at dinner or before bed.

- **Reframe challenges**: Even difficult moments can bring clarity, closeness, or lessons.

Caregiving Scenario: Patricia's Practice

Overwhelmed by caregiving, Patricia started jotting down simple gratitudes: "my morning coffee," "a quiet evening," "a good laugh". Over time, she began noticing more beauty in her day.

Action Step:

Start or end each day by writing three things you are grateful for, no matter how small.

H — Honor Your Feelings

Caregiving brings a broad spectrum of emotions: love, guilt, grief, frustration, and sometimes even resentment. All of them are valid. You do not need to suppress your feelings to be strong.

Why It is Important

Burying or dismissing emotions can lead to burnout. Instead, acknowledging your feelings can help you process them in healthy ways and find constructive outlets.

Ways to Honor Your Feelings:

- **Talk it out**: Confide in a friend, therapist, or support group.
- **Write it down**: Journaling gives your emotions a safe place to land.
- **Practice self-compassion**: Remind yourself that feeling overwhelmed does not mean you are failing.

Caregiving Scenario: Maureen's Release

Caring for her husband after a stroke, Maureen bottled up guilt and sadness until she finally confided in a friend. That honest conversation lifted a weight she did not even realize she was carrying.

Action Step:

Write down one emotion you've been avoiding. Give it a name, sit with it, and then explore what it is trying to teach you.

T — Think Positively

Positive thinking does not mean ignoring the hard stuff—it means consciously focusing on what you *can* control.

How to Cultivate a Positive Mindset:

- **Affirmations:** Say things like, "I am doing my best, and that is enough".

- **Solution-focused thinking:** When something goes wrong, ask, "What is one thing I can do right now?"

- **Surround yourself with light:** Read uplifting stories, listen to inspiring podcasts, and spend time with people who lift you up.

Caregiving Scenario: Earnest's Reframe

Earnest struggled with feeling "not good enough" as a caregiver. Using daily affirmations like, *"I am growing through this experience"* helped him face each day with renewed confidence.

Action Step:

Pick one positive affirmation that resonates with you. Say it each morning for the next 7 days and see how your energy shifts.

> "Caring in the shadows teaches us that even the smallest glimmers of light can guide us toward strength, hope, and clarity."

Chapter 6 Takeaways

- **Look for Small Wins**: Focus on progress, not perfection.

- **Incorporate Self-Care**: Small rituals can restore big energy.

- **Gratitude is key**: Practice seeing the good, even in the chaos.

- **Honor Your Feelings**: Your emotions are valid—give them space.

- **Think Positively**: Use affirmations and uplifting habits to stay grounded in hope.

Chapter 6 Reflection Questions

1. What small wins have you experienced recently in caregiving? How did they make you feel?

_____

_____

_____

_____

_____

_____

2. What self-care rituals could you realistically incorporate into your daily routine to restore your energy?

_____

_____

_____

_____

_____

_____

3. What are you most grateful for today—and how can you cultivate more moments of gratitude in your caregiving role?

_____

_____

_____

_____

_____

_____

The **L.I.G.H.T. Framework** is not about pretending everything is perfect. It is about bringing *intention, hope,* and *self-compassion* into your caregiving journey.

You deserve that light, and you are strong enough to shine through.

Breaking the Superwoman Cycle — Delegation as a B.O.S.S.

"True strength is not about doing it all; it's about knowing when to share the load."

Caregiving often comes with an unspoken expectation: you must handle everything yourself. You juggle caregiving, work, family responsibilities, and your personal life—all while trying to maintain the illusion of balance. But let's be honest: **trying to do it all leads straight to overwhelm and burnout.**

Breaking the "Superwoman Cycle" does not mean you are failing—it means you are **redefining success** by embracing delegation as a vital tool in your caregiving toolkit. Delegation is not giving up. It is a *power move*—prioritizing what matters most and preserving your energy for the long haul.

The **R.E.L.E.A.S.E. Strategy** is a step-by-step framework designed to help you let go of the need to do it all so that you can reclaim your health, peace, and time.

The R.E.L.E.A.S.E. strategy is not just a set of steps—it is a roadmap to reclaiming balance and well-being in your life as a caregiver. By implementing this strategy, you will move from a place of overwhelm to one of empowerment. Imagine what it would feel like to let go of the constant pressure to be everything to everyone. This strategy helps you create space for your own needs, improve your relationships, and enhance the quality of care you provide. Caregiving no longer means sacrificing your health, happiness, or peace of mind. Instead, you will learn how to share responsibilities, adapt to change, and approach caregiving with renewed strength and clarity. Let us break free from the Superwoman Cycle—one step at a time.

Why the Superwoman Cycle Has to End

Let's get real with the numbers:

- **66%** of caregivers are women.
- The average female caregiver provides **20+ hours** of care each week.
- **Up to 70%** experience symptoms of clinical depression.
- Female caregivers are **2.5x** more likely to live in poverty.
- **23%** report worsening health due to caregiving.

That is not just stressful—**it is dangerous.**

This cycle of over-functioning and under-supporting ourselves leads to chronic health issues, emotional exhaustion, and financial strain. It is not sustainable, and it is not necessary.

Caregiving Scenario: Linda's Wake-Up Call

Linda tried to manage her mother's care entirely alone—meals, cleaning, errands, and appointments. She ended up in hospital herself from pure exhaustion. Delegation became a necessity, not an option.

Delegating is not a weakness. It is wisdom.

The R.E.L.E.A.S.E. Strategy

This 7-step strategy helps you move from overwhelmed and overextended to supported and empowered:

- Recognize Your Limits
- Evaluate Your Resources
- Let Go of Guilt
- Enlist Support
- Accept Imperfection
- Set Boundaries
- Embrace Change

Let us walk through each step together.

R – Recognize Your Limits

Caregiving takes strength, but it also requires self-awareness. Ignoring your limits can lead to health decline, strained relationships, and emotional burnout.

Why It Matters: Recognizing your limits helps prevent burnout and potential chronic physical and mental health issues. When you know what is pushing you to the edge, you can address it before it becomes overwhelming. It is about being proactive, not reactive. Listen to your body and mind. They will tell you all you need to know.

How to Know Your Limits:

- Listen to your body: Are you constantly tired, irritable, or sick?
- Track your stress: What tasks leave you feeling emotionally drained?
- Reflect on your feelings: Are frustration or resentment creeping in?
- Ask trusted friends: They might see what you do not.

Consequences of Ignoring Limits: Failing to recognize your limits can lead to serious consequences. Burnout is a common outcome characterized by physical exhaustion, emotional detachment, and a reduced sense of accomplishment. Caregivers who ignore their limits are also at higher risk for chronic health conditions like heart disease and depression. Neglecting your own needs does not just affect you; it also impacts the quality of care you can provide. Over time, the lack of boundaries can strain relationships with loved ones and diminish your ability to enjoy life.

Caregiving Scenario: Joan's Turning Point

Joan, a caregiver for her mother, ignored her limits for months. She took on every task, from cooking and cleaning to managing medical appointments, without seeking help. Eventually, Joan's health began to decline, and she experienced frequent headaches and insomnia. Recognizing her limits became a turning point. She started using a meal delivery service and asked her sister to help with transportation. The result? Joan felt healthier and more present for her mother.

Action Step:

Write down your top three caregiving stressors. Which of these can be delegated, streamlined, or eliminated?

E – Evaluate Your Resources

Help is often closer than we think. Whether through community programs, technology, or family, **resources exist**—we just have to identify and access them.

Why It Matters: Many caregivers underestimate the variety of resources that can make their lives easier. Identifying these sources of support, from local community programs to online tools, can significantly reduce stress and free up valuable time. Proper evaluation ensures that you leverage all available options to lighten your caregiving load.

How to Evaluate Resources:

- **Map your network**: Who has offered help before? Who has a skill set you can tap into?

- **Explore local services:** Senior centers, libraries, churches, and nonprofits offer everything from transportation to respite care.

- **Use apps and tools:** Digital calendars, medication trackers, and caregiver apps can simplify your day.

- **Talk to professionals:** Ask social workers or doctors about services you may not know exist.

Caregiving Scenario: Maria's Discovery

When Maria became the primary caregiver for her father after his stroke, she felt overwhelmed with managing his medical appointments, meals, and household chores. A friend suggested that Maria explore local community resources. She discovered a nearby senior center that offered free transportation to medical appointments and a subsidized meal delivery program. By using these services, Maria saved hours each week, giving her time to focus on her father's emotional needs and her self-care. She also joined a caregiver support group at the center, gaining valuable insights and a sense of connection with others in similar situations.

Action Step:

Start by choosing one area where you feel overwhelmed, such as transportation or meal preparation. Research at least two available resources to help address that need this week.

L – Let Go of Guilt

Letting go of guilt starts with acknowledging that you are human, not a superhero, and that caregiving is an act of love, not perfection. Guilt often stems from the unrealistic expectation that you must do it all, never make mistakes, and never feel frustrated or tired. However, holding onto this guilt only drains your emotional energy and clouds your ability to make clear decisions.

Caregiving guilt can be paralyzing. Letting go of the belief that, "I have to do everything" frees you to accept help without shame.

Why It Matters: Guilt keeps caregivers stuck in a cycle of self-blame and overextension. It prevents you from asking for help, delegating tasks, or taking breaks when needed. Over time, this emotional burden can lead to burnout, strained relationships, and even health problems. Letting go of guilt frees you to prioritize sustainable care for both your loved one and yourself.

Mindset Shift: Reframe guilt as a signal that you care deeply. Instead of letting it weigh you down, use it as a reminder to act in ways that preserve your well-being. Sharing responsibilities does not mean you care less; it means you are ensuring that your care is effective and sustainable.

How to Release Guilt:

- Name it: "I feel guilty because…"
- Challenge it: Would you expect this of a friend in your shoes?
- Reframe it: Guilt means you care, not that you are failing.
- Replace it: Affirm yourself: "I am doing my best, and that is enough."

Action Step:

Choose one caregiving task you have hesitated to delegate because of guilt. Ask for help—and notice how that one shift lightens your emotional and physical load.

E – Enlist Support

Enlisting support is about recognizing that caregiving does not have to be a solo journey. By reaching out and involving others, you build a network of assistance that lightens your load and ensures your loved one receives the best care possible. Asking for help is not a sign of failure; it's an act of strength and foresight.

Reach out to others and clearly communicate your needs. Be specific about the tasks you would like help with and who could assist.

Why It Matters: Support networks are essential for sustainable caregiving. Trying to do everything yourself can lead to burnout, resentment, and decreased quality of care. When you enlist others, you share responsibilities and create opportunities for others to connect with your loved one and support you emotionally.

How to Enlist Help:

- Make a list of people who might be willing to help.
- Be specific: "Can you bring groceries this Saturday?"
- Use technology: Shared calendars, messaging apps, and care coordination tools.

- Accept help in all forms: Some can give time, others financial or emotional support.

- Show appreciation: Gratitude fuels continued connection.

Caregiving Scenario: Tina's Teamwork

Tina's sister lived out of state but wanted to help. Tina asked her to manage their dad's financial paperwork online, which saved Tina hours each month. Additionally, a neighbor offered to assist with weekly grocery shopping, further lightening Tina's load and allowing her to focus on her father's emotional well-being.

Action Step:

Pick one task you can hand off this week. Be clear, kind, and specific. Notice how you feel after letting someone else take the wheel.

A – Accept Imperfection

Accepting imperfection means shifting your focus from how things are done to the results that truly matter. As caregivers, it is easy to become fixated on perfection, believing that everything must be done your way to be done right: the "If you want something done right, do it yourself!" attitude. However, this mindset can lead to unnecessary stress and limit your ability to delegate effectively. By letting go of the need for flawless execution, you open yourself up to support, creativity, and more time for what matters most: your loved one's well-being and your peace of mind.

Why It Matters: Perfectionism often leads to micromanagement, leaving you exhausted and overwhelmed. When you focus less on how tasks are completed and more on whether they achieve the desired outcome, you create room for others to help. This approach fosters collaboration, reduces stress, and ensures that caregiving remains sustainable over time. The key is recognizing that the value lies in the results, not in the process.

How to Embrace "Good Enough":

- Focus on outcomes, not methods.

- Practice releasing control on one small task (like folding laundry).

- Celebrate effort over flawlessness.

- Recognize that imperfection does not equal failure.

Caregiving Scenario: Lisa's Lightbulb Moment

Lisa delegated her dad's laundry to her teenage son. At first, she worried about how neatly the clothes would be folded, but she reminded herself that having clean laundry was the priority, not perfect folds. When Lisa saw how much time and energy she saved, she felt relief and realized that small imperfections did not detract from the overall care her dad received. This simple act of letting go allowed her to focus on spending meaningful time with her father.

Action Step:

Choose one task to delegate this week. Let someone else do it—and resist the urge to "fix" it.

S – Set Boundaries

- Setting boundaries is essential for maintaining your emotional and physical health as a caregiver. It is not about being selfish but preserving your ability to care effectively while protecting your well-being. Boundaries create clarity in your relationships, ensuring that everyone understands your limits and respects your time and energy.

- **Why It Matters:** Without boundaries, caregivers can quickly become overwhelmed, leading to burnout, resentment, and compromised care. Boundaries allow you to prioritize what is most important, avoid unnecessary stress, and maintain a sense of control over your life. They also model healthy behavior for others, encouraging mutual respect and understanding.

How to Set Healthy Boundaries:

- Identify your stress points: Late-night calls? Unreasonable asks?
- Communicate clearly: "I am unavailable after 8 p.m. for caregiving tasks."
- Expect pushback—and hold your ground.
- Re-evaluate often: Life shifts, and your boundaries should too.

Scenario: Rachel Takes Control

Rachel, a caregiver for her father, found herself constantly dealing with late-night phone calls from extended family members asking for updates. These calls disrupted her sleep and added to her stress. Rachel set a clear boundary by designating a specific weekly time to provide family updates. This enabled her to get adequate rest and streamlined communication, reducing misunderstandings and frustration.

Action Step:

Set one boundary this week. Whether it is saying "no" to a task or setting office hours for caregiving questions, stick to it and feel the freedom.

E – Embrace Change

Caregiving is a constantly evolving journey; embracing change is essential to navigating twists and turns. Change can feel overwhelming, but it also brings opportunities for growth, innovation, and improved caregiving strategies. The ability to adapt is not just a survival skill; it is a superpower that allows you to thrive amidst uncertainty.

Why It Matters: Resistance to change can lead to frustration, inefficiency, and missed opportunities for improvement. When you embrace change, you become more open to discovering tools, resources, and strategies that make caregiving more manageable. Adapting to change also helps you maintain emotional resilience, which is critical for long-term caregiving.

How to Adapt:

- Acknowledge resistance: What are you afraid of losing by changing?

- Try one new thing: An app, a support group, or telehealth visits.

- Focus on the benefits: Will this save time? Ease stress? Improve connection?

- Celebrate the wins—even the small ones.

Caregiving Scenario: Bobbi's Tech Pivot

After years of managing all aspects of her father's care alone, Bobbi hesitated to explore telehealth options for her father's frequent medical checkups. She worried it would lack the personal touch of in-person visits. However, after trying it, she realized how much time and stress it saved— not just for her but also for her father, who appreciated avoiding lengthy trips to the clinic. Embracing this change improved their quality of life and freed up valuable time for rest and connection.

Action Step:

Identify one caregiving challenge you've been tackling with outdated methods. Research a new solution and commit to trying it this week.

> "Delegation isn't about letting go of responsibility; it's about sharing the journey so you can walk farther together."

Chapter 7 Takeaways

- **Caregiving is not a solo act:** Delegation empowers both you and your loved one.

- **Know your limits:** You cannot give your best if you are burned out.

- **Leverage your resources:** Help is out there—you just have to access it.

- **Let go of guilt:** You are human, not a machine.

- **Accept imperfection:** Done is better than perfect.

- **Set boundaries:** Your time and energy deserve protection.

- **Embrace change:** Flexibility is your caregiving superpower.

Chapter 7 Reflection Questions

1. What caregiving tasks are you currently trying to manage on your own, and how is it affecting you—physically, mentally, or emotionally?

    _____

    _____

    _____

    _____

    _____

2. Who in your life could you reach out to for support or assistance with caregiving responsibilities?

    _____

    _____

    _____

    _____

    _____

3. What is one task you can delegate this week—and how will doing so free up time, energy, or peace for yourself?

    _____

    _____

    _____

    _____

The Superwoman Cycle is unsustainable.

Delegation is not giving up—it is showing up. Wiser, stronger, and more sustainably.

Permission to Pause — Finding Time for Yourself

> "Pausing is not stepping away from caregiving; it's stepping toward sustainability."

When did you last do something just for yourself, without feeling guilty about it? If you have to think for too long, this chapter is certainly for you!

Caregiving can feel all-consuming, leaving little room for rest or renewal. One of the most common things I hear from caregivers is, **"I do not have time for self-care"**.

But here is the truth: That mindset is a trap. It fuels burnout, deepens exhaustion, and quietly convinces you that you do not matter.

This chapter is your reminder—and your *permission slip*—to pause. To rest. To *be*. Not just because you have earned it by running yourself ragged, but because you are human and you deserve it.

Finding Time for Yourself

Finding time starts with prioritizing your needs alongside your caregiving responsibilities. Self-care is not selfish. It is an investment in your ability to keep going.

A 2020 study by the National Alliance for Caregiving revealed:

- **23%** of family caregivers reported a decline in their health.
- **Over 40%** experienced high levels of emotional stress.

Even 10 minutes of stillness can transform your day. The key? Intention.

The Benefits of Making Time for Yourself

When you pause, you restore. These benefits ripple across every part of your life—from your health to your relationships to your peace of mind.

What the Pause Can Do:

- **Boost Mental Health**: Reduces stress, lowers anxiety, and brings emotional clarity.
- **Support Physical Wellness**: Improves sleep, reduces blood pressure, lowers burnout risk.
- **Increase Patience and Focus**: Helps you show up calmer and more present.
- **Strengthen Relationships**: A well-rested caregiver connects more deeply with loved ones.

The Cost of Neglecting Yourself

Ignoring your needs does not make you a better caregiver. It just makes you exhausted, and exhaustion has consequences.

Risks of Skipping Self-Care:

- **Burnout**: Emotional detachment, irritability, and compassion fatigue

- **Chronic Health Issues**: Increased risk of hypertension, diabetes, and low immunity

- **Mental Health Decline**: Higher rates of anxiety, depression, and isolation

- **Strained Relationships**: Unspoken resentment and depleted emotional availability

Practical Steps to Reclaim Time

Let's make self-care doable, not daunting. Here is how to start, one small pause at a time:

1. Reframe Your Mindset

Swap *"I don't have time"* for *"I will make time"*. Even five minutes matter. Remember, you are not just pausing but also protecting your capacity to keep going.

2. Use Pockets of Time

Identify opportunities throughout the day to pause. While waiting for an appointment or during your loved one's nap, take a few moments to breathe deeply or enjoy a brief activity that brings you joy.

3. Create Rituals

Simple routines create structure:

- Tea before bed

- Morning music or gratitude journaling

- Five-minute stretches when you wake up

4. Combine Tasks with Joy

- Listen to music while doing chores.

- Watch a favorite show with your loved one.

- Dance while folding laundry—yes, really!

5. Ask for Help

- You are not alone. Enlist help from friends, family, or professional services—even if just for an hour. Use that time to refuel, not catch up on chores.

Recognizing the Signs of Burnout

Burnout does not show up overnight—it builds. *Pay attention to the whispers before they become shouts.*

Common Signs Include:

- Persistent fatigue

- Feeling emotionally numb or constantly on edge

- Losing interest in things you once enjoyed

- Difficulty making decisions or staying focused

- Neglecting your own health and appointments

If any of these signs sound familiar, it is time to pause—*not later, NOW.*

Quick Stats to Consider:

- **Over 60%** of caregivers report elevated stress levels (AARP, 2023)

- **40%** of caregivers rarely feel relaxed (AARP, 2023 Caregiver Mental Health Report)

- Only **1 in 5** caregivers rate themselves highly at exercising (Guardian Life, 2023 Caregiving in America Report)

- **72%** experience emotional stress from job-caregiving balance (AARP Vermont 2024)

These are not just numbers. They are red flags—and reasons to choose rest today.

"In the act of pausing, you give yourself the strength to keep going."

Chapter 8 Takeaways

- **Prioritize Self-Care**: You matter—your rest is part of the care you provide.

- **Small Steps Count**: Even 10 minutes of calm can shift your mood and energy.

- **Spot Burnout Early**: Know the signs, and do not ignore them.

- **Integrate, Do Not Add**: Blend self-care into your routine—it does not need to be "one more thing".

- **Build Resilience**: Pauses are how you refill your cup and keep going strong.

Chapter 8 Reflection Questions

1. When was the last time you truly took time for yourself? How did it make you feel?

   _____

   _____

   _____

   _____

   _____

   _____

2. What barriers keep you from prioritizing rest, and how can you gently shift them?

   _____

   _____

   _____

   _____

   _____

3. What is one small, intentional pause you can take today to renew your energy?

   _____

   _____

   _____

   _____

   _____

You cannot pour from an empty cup—and you were never meant to.

The Caregiver's Compass — Finding Your North Star

"When your caregiving aligns with your values, even the hardest tasks feel more meaningful."

Your North Star is your guiding purpose—the deep motivation that keeps you going when caregiving feels heavy and hard. It is the quiet reminder of why you show up every day, even when it feels like too much.

Caregiving is inherently complex. It is filled with unexpected turns, emotional landmines, and moments where you question everything. It can feel even more burdensome for caregivers who stepped into this role out of obligation rather than choice.

But here is the thing: **everything shifts when you reconnect with your "why"—your personal North Star**. Purpose breathes life into routine. *It transforms obligation into intention*. It gives weight to the small moments and meaning to the hard ones.

So, let's get clear on *your* North Star—and how it can anchor you through even the most difficult periods.

For the Reluctant Caregiver: Finding Purpose When It Wasn't Your Choice

Let's be honest—not all caregivers choose this role. Sometimes it is handed to us because there is no one else. Maybe it came from a sense of duty, family expectations, cultural norms, or simply because "you are the responsible one".

And with these situations can come **conflicting emotions**: guilt, resentment, and overwhelm. These emotions do not make you a bad caregiver by the way—they make you human.

Ways to Find Purpose Through the Fog:

- **Shift your perspective**: Instead of focusing on what you've lost (freedom, time, etc.), ask what you might gain—resilience, strength, deeper compassion.

- **Set personal goals**: Caregiving can help you become more organized, deepen family ties, or develop skills you never thought had or would need.

- **Look for small joys**: a shared laugh, a favorite song, or a photo that brings back a warm memory.

Caregiving Scenario: Jamie's Journal

Jamie did not choose to care for her father—it just happened. She started journaling each night, listing one thing she was grateful for. Over time, her lens shifted. She found beauty in the quiet moments, like sorting old photos together, and slowly, resentment was replaced with meaning.

Aligning Caregiving with Your Values

Values are the foundation of purpose. When your caregiving aligns with what matters most to you, it feels like an extension of who you are, not just something you do.

Steps to Align Your Care with Your Values:

- **Identify your core values**
  - What drives you most? Is it family, compassion, independence, spirituality, justice, kindness?

- **Ask how caregiving supports those values**
  - If you value family, caregiving might reflect your commitment to legacy and loyalty.
  - If you value integrity, providing dignified care could affirm your principles.

- **Reframe the mundane**
  - That load of laundry? It is an act of love.
  - That doctor's appointment? A symbol of your reliability and care.

- **Adjust misalignments**
  - If something feels off, ask: Can I delegate this? Can I do it differently to make it feel more meaningful?

Caregiving Scenario: Rose's Knowledge Shift

Rose, a lifelong learner, found caregiving repetitive—until she started researching her mother's diagnosis. She immersed herself in learning, joined a support group, and became a confident advocate in care meetings. Her value of education infused purpose into her role.

Creating a Vision for Caregiving

A caregiving *vision* helps you move from surviving to thriving. It is not about perfection—it's about **clarity and direction**. What do you want caregiving to feel like? What do you want to preserve for yourself along the way?

How to Create Your Vision:

- **Visualize your ideal caregiving life**
    - What does balance look like? Are you finding time for yourself? Laughing with your loved one? Feeling supported?

- **Set small, practical goals**
    - Weekly walks
    - Monthly family check-ins
    - Boundaries for alone time

- **Include your growth**
    - Is caregiving making you more patient? Creative? Stronger?

- **Stay flexible**
    - Your needs and circumstances will evolve—let your vision evolve too.

Caregiving Scenario: Carla's Connection

Carla envisioned caregiving as a shared family journey. She started organizing monthly Zoom calls with siblings to update care plans. That sense of teamwork reduced her burden and deepened her relationship with her mom, especially during their gardening sessions together.

> "When you find your North Star, caregiving becomes more than a responsibility—it becomes a reflection of who you are and what you stand for."

Chapter 9 Takeaways

- **Acknowledge Your Feelings:** It's okay to feel unsure, tired, or reluctant. Honoring your truth is the first step toward healing and purpose.

- **Reconnect with Your Values:** Aligning daily caregiving with what matters most to you brings meaning, even in the most mundane of tasks.

- **Reframe the Experience:** Purpose is not always about grandeur— it lives in the small, meaningful wins.

- **Create a Vision:** Permit yourself to imagine and visualize a caregiving life that includes peace, joy, and self-care.

- **Celebrate the Moments:** Every act of care is a reflection of love. Let those moments matter.

Chapter 9 Reflection Questions

1. What are your core values, and how do they influence your approach to caregiving?

   _____

   _____

   _____

   _____

   _____

2. How can you reframe caregiving tasks to align more closely with your values and purpose?

   _____

   _____

   _____

   _____

   _____

   _____

3. What does your caregiving "North Star" look like—and how does it guide your daily actions?

   _____

   _____

   _____

   _____

   _____

Let Your North Star guide you through the storm.

Leading With Grace –
Your B.O.S.S. Caregiver Legacy

"Legacy is not what you leave behind, but the love, strength, and lessons you imprint on the lives you touch."

Your legacy is about so much more than the tasks you complete as a caregiver. It is the lasting imprint of your compassion, consistency, and quiet strength. Your legacy is built in the everyday moments—in the sacrifices, comfort, and hope you pass along to others who watch you navigate it all.

Accolades do not measure legacy. Legacy is measured by impact.

It is reflected in the relationships you nurture, the lessons you live out, and the example you set for others. When you lead with grace and balance, your influence ripples outward, touching not only your loved one but your family, your community, and generations to come.

Why Legacy Matters

- **It shapes future generations**

  Your caregiving example teaches others how to embody compassion, responsibility, and emotional resilience.

- **It brings clarity to your actions**

  Reflecting on the kind of legacy you want to leave helps you align your daily efforts with your deepest values.

- **It offers fulfillment**

  Knowing your care leaves a positive mark brings meaning to the most challenging aspects of caregiving.

Pause and Reflect: What Will Your Legacy Be?

Take a moment to ask yourself:

- How do I want my loved one to remember the care I gave?

- What example do I want to set for others who may one day walk this path?

- How can I ensure my caregiving reflects the values I hold dear?

Your legacy is not about perfection. It is about consistency, intention, and love.

How Caregiving Has Shaped Your Life and Relationships

Caregiving has likely changed you in ways both visible and invisible. Maybe it has taught you to have patience amid chaos or strength during uncertainty. Maybe it has helped you find your voice—or remember your worth.

Whether you chose this path or were placed on it unexpectedly, your caregiving journey has shaped how you show up in the world.

Reflection Prompt

Write down three ways caregiving has changed you. Here are some examples:

- I have become more empathetic.

- I have learned to set boundaries.

- I have grown closer to my family.

Now reflect on how these changes have influenced your relationships. Are you more present, more honest, more intentional? Those are parts of your legacy, too.

Crafting Your Caregiver Story

Your story matters. It is a living testimony of love, sacrifice, and growth. When you share it—privately or publicly—you permit others to honor their journeys, too.

How to Craft Your Story

1. **Identify key moments**

   What turning points shaped your experience? What was hard? What was beautiful?

2. **Highlight your growth**

   How have you changed? What strengths have emerged?

3. **Connect to a broader message**

   What universal truths does your story hold? Perhaps it's about perseverance, vulnerability, or rediscovering self-worth.

4. **Be honest**

   Perfection does not inspire—authenticity does. Share your highs and lows, your doubts and breakthroughs.

Caregiving Scenario: Caroline's Story

Caroline began caring for her father after his stroke. At first, she felt overwhelmed and isolated. Over time, she learned to ask for help, set healthy boundaries, and find joy in the little moments. Sharing her story in a caregiver group gave her purpose—and reminded her just how far she'd come.

Action Step

Write a one-page reflection on your caregiving journey. Focus on the moments that taught you something or changed your perspective. Consider sharing it with someone in your circle or keeping it as a reminder of your strength.

Embracing the Lessons and Looking Ahead with Hope

Caregiving is about helping someone else and uncovering who you are under pressure, in love, and through growth.

Lessons to Carry Forward

- **Resilience:** You have faced what once felt impossible—and found a way through. This skill will help you in the other inevitable challenges in your life.

- **Adaptability:** You have pivoted more times than you can count. That flexibility is a life skill that will serve you beyond caregiving.

- **Compassion:** You have often practiced empathy, patience, and kindness when it was hardest to do so. This will benefit all your relationships.

Looking Ahead

Now is the time to consider how your caregiving journey can shape your next chapter. Maybe you will:

- Mentor a new caregiver.

- Advocate for better resources.

- Simply honor the wisdom you have earned.

Scenario: Barbara's New Chapter

Barbara began volunteering at a local senior center when her caregiving journey ended. She shared insights from her experience and helped other families navigate similar paths. It became a way to honor her mother and continue making a difference.

Chapter 10 Takeaways

- **Reflect on Growth:** Caregiving has shaped you—mentally, emotionally, spiritually. Honor that.

- **Tell Your Story:** You do not have to be a writer to make an impact. Share your journey with honesty and heart.

- **Embrace the Lessons:** Resilience, adaptability, compassion— these are the gifts caregiving leaves you with.

- **Plan Your Next Chapter:** Your experience has value. Use it to uplift, support, or transform the lives of others.

- **Live Your Legacy:** Legacy is not about what you do once but how you live every day. Lead with grace. Let your care speak volumes.

Your caregiving legacy is not just about the care you provide but about the lessons you carry forward and the inspiration you offer others. By leading with grace, you ensure that your journey becomes a beacon of hope for those who follow.

Chapter 10 Reflection Questions

1. What do you hope your caregiving legacy will be, and how do you want to be remembered by your loved ones?

    _____

    _____

    _____

    _____

    _____

2. How has caregiving shaped your personal growth, relationships, and outlook on life?

    _____

    _____

    _____

    _____

    _____

3. What lessons from your caregiving journey can you share to inspire or guide others?

    _____

    _____

    _____

    _____

    _____

You have made it through hard days, long nights, impossible decisions, and countless small moments that no one else may ever see.

Through it all, you have given something beautiful—your presence.

Take a deep breath. Place your hand over your heart, and remind yourself:

You have made a difference.

Not because it was easy.

Not because it was perfect.

But because you showed up with love, grace, and grit.

That is your legacy, and it will echo far beyond today.

Your Next Step as a B.O.S.S. Caregiver

"Your legacy isn't just what you leave behind—it's how you choose to lead today."

As you reach the end of this book, let me remind you: caregiving is not just about the tasks you complete; it is about the lives you touch, especially your own. You have navigated the pages of this journey with courage, reflection, and a willingness to grow. Now, it is time to move from learning to action.

Being a B.O.S.S. caregiver is about more than balancing obligations, supporting others, and prioritizing self-care. It is about leading with intention and leaving behind a legacy rooted in strength, love, and resilience. This is your moment to take everything you have absorbed and begin applying it in a way that empowers both you and those around you.

Small Steps Lead to Big Change

You do not have to overhaul your entire life to make a difference. In fact, the most powerful transformations begin with the smallest of steps. Identify one area where you can apply the tools and frameworks from this book. It could be delegating more using the S.H.A.R.E. framework or incorporating the L.I.G.H.T. framework as a self-care guide. *Whatever calls you,* **choose one change and start today.**

Remember, progress is built one intentional action at a time. Perfection is not the goal—the goal is sustainability.

Build Your Support Network

One of the most important truths I can leave you with is this: you are not alone. The caregiving journey was not meant to be walked in isolation. Lean into your support system, build your circle, and reach out when needed. Whether it is family, friends, faith communities, or professional services, there is help, and you deserve to receive it.

Use the strategies in this book to uplift not just yourself, but also those walking alongside you. Together, we create a movement of caregivers who thrive, not just survive.

Embrace Your Legacy

You have shown up with love, led with grace, and grown in ways you never thought possible. That is the foundation of your legacy.

Let your caregiving journey be a testament to your strength, compassion, and purpose. When you lead with intention and share what you have learned, you empower others to do the same. That ripple effect? It is how your legacy will live on long after the caregiving chapter ends.

Your Call to Action

Take one bold, deliberate step today. Reflect on your values. Set a new boundary. Share your story. Or simply pause and breathe in the truth that you've made it this far—and that is worth celebrating.

You are not just a caregiver. You are a B.O.S.S.—a leader, a nurturer, and a source of light for your loved one and your community. Lead boldly. Care deeply. And continue to thrive.

Your legacy starts now

Frequently Asked
Questions and Common Challenges

As you continue navigating your caregiving journey, you may find questions you need answers to as you face new obstacles. You are not alone. Below are some of the most common concerns caregivers share, along with practical solutions, resources, and words of encouragement to help you move forward with confidence.

Frequently Asked Questions (FAQ)

Q1: What is the B.O.S.S. mindset, and how can it help me?

The B.O.S.S. mindset stands for Balancing Obligation, Supporting, and Self-Care. It's a framework designed to help caregivers manage their responsibilities without losing sight of their own well-being. By focusing on balance, seeking support, and prioritizing self-care, caregivers can create a more sustainable and fulfilling caregiving experience.

Q2: How can I manage caregiving responsibilities without burning out?

Burnout prevention starts with recognizing your limits and making self-care a priority. Use tools like the S.H.A.R.E. framework to delegate tasks and build a support network. Incorporate daily pauses for mindfulness, gratitude, or rest. Small, consistent acts of self-care can make a big difference.

Q3: What should I do if I feel guilty about taking breaks or asking for help?

Guilt is a familiar feeling among caregivers, but it is important to reframe it. Taking breaks and seeking help are acts of strength, not selfishness. Remember, you cannot pour from an empty cup. By caring for yourself, you are ensuring you can continue providing the best possible care for your loved one.

Q4: How can I balance caregiving with work and other responsibilities?

Time management and setting clear boundaries are key. Use tools like caregiving schedules, checklists, and technology to stay organized. Communicate openly with your employer about your caregiving role and explore flexible work arrangements. Do not hesitate to delegate tasks to others in your support circle.

Q5: What are some resources I can use as a caregiver?

National organizations such as: the Family Caregiver Alliance and AARP Caregiving Resource Center provide valuable tools and support. Apps including Medisafe and CaringBridge can help with medication management and communication. Check local senior centers or Area Agencies on Aging for community-specific resources.

Common Challenges and Solutions

Challenge 1: Feeling Overwhelmed by Responsibilities

Solution: Break tasks into smaller, manageable steps and prioritize the most critical ones. Use the L.I.G.H.T. framework to focus on small wins and incorporate self-care into your daily routine. Delegate tasks whenever possible using the R.E.L.E.A.S.E. strategy.

Challenge 2: Lack of Support from Family or Friends

Solution: Clearly communicate your needs and use specific requests when asking for help. If your immediate circle is unavailable, explore community resources, hire professional services, or join a caregiver support group to connect with others who understand your journey.

Challenge 3: Struggling to Set Boundaries

Solution: Use the P.A.U.S.E. method to establish and maintain healthy boundaries. Practice assertive communication, anticipate pushback, and stay consistent. Remember, boundaries protect your energy and enhance the quality of care you provide.

Challenge 4: Navigating Complex Emotions Like Guilt or Resentment

Solution: Honor your feelings by acknowledging them without judgment. Journaling, talking to a trusted friend, or seeking therapy can help process these emotions. Focus on the positive impact of your caregiving role and celebrate your efforts, even when they feel small.

Challenge 5: Managing a Loved One's Changing Needs

Solution: Stay adaptable by regularly evaluating your caregiving approach. Use the C.A.R.E. framework to understand the level of care required and adjust your strategies as needed. Leverage professional advice or support groups to navigate transitions more smoothly.

Challenge 6: Feeling Isolated or Disconnected

Solution: Combat isolation by staying connected with friends, family, or support groups. Schedule regular check-ins with your support circle and explore virtual communities for caregivers. Do not hesitate to share your story—it can foster connection and inspire others.

Challenge 7: Balancing Personal Goals with Caregiving Demands

Solution: Create a vision for caregiving that incorporates your aspirations. Set small, achievable goals that align with your values and caregiving responsibilities. Use time-blocking techniques to ensure you carve out space for growth and happiness.

Final Note

Remember, caregiving is a journey, not a destination. Challenges will arise, but with the right tools, mindset, and support, you can navigate them with grace and resilience. You are not alone—every step you take toward balance and well-being is a step toward a brighter caregiving experience.

The Caregiver's Resource Directory

> "You don't have to do it all alone—support is out there, and this directory is a great place to start."

This directory is designed to be your go-to guide for trusted tools, hotlines, organizations, and community resources. Whether you seek education, emotional support, or technology that simplifies your day-to-day life, these resources can help you feel more equipped and less isolated.

National Resources

Family Caregiver Alliance (FCA)

🌐 caregiver.org

Comprehensive education, fact sheets, and tailored caregiver support programs.

AARP Caregiving Resource Center

🌐 aarp.org/caregiving

Expert advice, checklists, and a caregiver community for connection and practical tips.

Alzheimer's Association

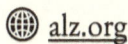 alz.org

24/7 helpline, educational tools, and support groups for dementia and Alzheimer's caregivers.

National Alliance for Caregiving (NAC)

⊕ caregiving.org

Offers cutting-edge research, advocacy, and caregiver policy resources.

Local Resources

Area Agencies on Aging (AAA)

⊕ eldercare.acl.gov

Connects you with local services like transportation, meal delivery, respite care, and caregiver training.

Faith-Based Support

Many churches, mosques, and synagogues offer volunteer ministries for caregivers, including help with errands, meals, or prayer support.

Community Centers

Check with your local recreation or community center for caregiver workshops, support groups, or respite programs tailored to your area.

Technology Tools & Apps

CaringBridge

🌐 caringbridge.org

Create a private site to update and communicate with family to coordinate meals, visits, or care needs.

Medisafe

🌐 medisafeapp.com

Track medications, set reminders, and keep everyone on the care team in sync.

Hero Health

🌐 herohealth.com

automated medication dispenser and smart reminder system that is helpful to support medication adherence.

Lotsa Helping Hands

🌐 lotsahelpinghands.com

Build a care calendar and recruit family and friends to help with meals, rides, and errands.

Caregiver Action Network (CAN)

🌐 caregiveraction.org

Offers peer support, free online education, and a downloadable resource toolbox

Hotlines & Immediate Support

National Suicide & Crisis Lifeline

📞 Dial **988** (24/7)

Confidential support for anyone in distress—whether caregiver or care recipient.

Alzheimer's Association Helpline

📞 1-800-272-3900 (24/7)

Live support and answers to dementia-related questions, any time.

Elder Abuse Hotline (Eldercare Locator)

📞 1-800-677-1116

Find state-specific reporting agencies and safety resources.

SAMHSA National Helpline

📞 1-800-662-HELP (4357)

Free, confidential guidance on mental health and substance use services.

References

This list includes the key resources and references used to support the insights, frameworks, and recommendations throughout *The B.O.S.S. Caregiver: Balancing Life, Love, and Self-Care with Grace.*

National Organizations & Government Agencies

Family Caregiver Alliance (FCA)

Website: https://www.caregiver.org

Offers comprehensive resources for family caregivers, including fact sheets, evidence-based programs, and advocacy tools.

National Alliance for Caregiving (NAC)

Website: https://www.caregiving.org

Publishes leading national research and provides tools for advocacy and public policy.

AARP Caregiving Resource Center

Website: https://www.aarp.org/caregiving

Provides expert guidance, checklists, articles, and planning tools for family caregivers.

Alzheimer's Association

Website: https://www.alz.org

Offers resources & a 24/7 support line for Alzheimer's and dementia caregiving.

Centers for Disease Control and Prevention (CDC)

Website: https://www.cdc.gov

Provides research & public health stats on caregiver-related stress & chronic conditions.

National Institute on Aging (NIA)

Website: https://www.nia.nih.gov

Features evidence-based articles and health tips for caregivers of aging adults.

Caregiver Action Network (CAN)

Website: https://www.caregiveraction.org

Offers educational resources, peer support, and a directory of national caregiver support agencies.

Caregiving Statistics and Research

Family Caregiver Alliance (2022). *Caregiver statistics: Demographics.* https://www.caregiver.org/resource/caregiver-statistics-demographics/

Family Caregiver Alliance (2024). *Best programs for caregiving.* https://www.caregiver.org/professional-resources/best-programs-for-caregiving/

Family Caregiving Institute, Betty Irene Moore School of Nursing, UC Davis Health (n.d.). *Family caregiving research.*
https://health.ucdavis.edu/family-caregiving/research/

National Alliance for Caregiving & AARP (2020). *Caregiving in the U.S. 2020.*
https://www.caregiver.org/research/caregiving-in-the-us/

AARP (2023). *A look at U.S. caregivers' mental health.*
https://www.aarp.org/caregiving/health/info-2023/report-caregiver-mental-health.html

Guardian Life Insurance Company of America (2023). *Standing up and stepping in: A modern look at caregivers in the U.S.*
https://www.guardianlife.com/reports/caregiving-in-america

AARP (2024). *Working while caregiving: It's complicated.*
https://www.aarp.org/caregiving/life-balance/info-2024/working-caregivers-report.html

Books and
Recommended Reading

Mace, N. L., & Rabins, P. V. (2020). *The 36-Hour Day: A Family Guide to Caring for People Who Have Alzheimer's Disease, Other Dementias, and Memory Loss.* Baltimore: Johns Hopkins University Press.

Sheehy, G. (2010). *Passages in Caregiving: Turning Chaos into Confidence.* New York: HarperCollins.

Blight, A. (2020). *When Caregiving Calls: Guidance as You Care for a Parent, Spouse, or Aging Relative.* Tallahassee, FL: Author Academy Elite.

FitzPatrick, J. L. (2015). *Cruising through Caregiving: Reducing the Stress of Caring for Your Loved One.* Greenleaf Book Group Press.

Boss, P. (2011). *Loving Someone Who Has Dementia: How to Find Hope While Coping with Stress and Grief.* San Francisco: Jossey-Bass.

Gawande, A. (2014). *Being Mortal: Medicine and What Matters in the End.* New York: Metropolitan Books.

Daily Caring (2024). *12 Top Books for Caregiver Advice and Support.*
Retrieved from: https://dailycaring.com/9-top-caregiver-support-books-for-stress-relief/

AgingCare.com. (2021). *Must-Read Books for Caregivers.*
Retrieved from:

Academic Journals and Articles

Journal of Gerontology
Website: https://academic.oup.com/gerontologist
Peer-reviewed research on aging and caregiving.

Journal of Applied Gerontology
Website: https://journals.sagepub.com/home/jag
Applied research on caregiving practices, interventions, and policies.

Acknowledgments

This book would not have been possible without my family's and friends' unwavering support and love. Your encouragement and belief in me have guided me throughout this journey. Thank you for standing by me during the long nights, the moments of self-doubt, and the countless hours of writing and reflection. Your presence in my life is my greatest blessing.

To my husband, thank you for always being my steady place, my encourager, and my biggest supporter. Your love, patience, and belief in me have carried me through the highs and lows of this journey. I am forever grateful and blessed to walk through life and purpose by your side.

To my personal experiences and the caregiving moments I have witnessed from afar that have quietly shaped my understanding - thank you for inspiring the pages of this book. Your journey of caregiving, love, and dedication helped shape the frameworks and insights within these chapters.

Special thanks to Joyce Challis for your editorial support and detailed suggestions. Your input added polish to every page.

Finally, to you, the reader: thank you for taking this step to invest in your caregiving journey. This book provides you with tools, encouragement, and renewed hope. Remember, you are not alone. Your situation can improve, and your efforts make an extraordinary difference in the lives of those you care for.

About the Author

L.P. Golphin, affectionately known as LeLe G, is a dedicated nurse, licensed social worker, educator, and board-certified psychiatric nurse with over 20 years of experience in case management and caregiving advocacy. As the founder and CEO of Remedy Senior Care Concierge, she has made it her mission to empower family caregivers by providing practical solutions, emotional support, and innovative strategies to help them navigate the complexities of caregiving with confidence.

Inspired by her journey supporting her mother, offering emotional encouragement, financial help, and assistance with errands, and informed by her professional expertise in healthcare, LeLe blends compassion, resilience, and practical wisdom to guide caregivers through one of life's most challenging roles. Her work focuses on helping busy working women, especially those in the "sandwich generation" find balance, prioritize self-care, and build a strong support network to thrive while caring for their loved ones.

A passionate advocate for integrating technology and AI into caregiving, LeLe offers workshops and coaching programs to teach caregivers how to simplify routines and lighten their load using modern tools. When she's not writing, speaking, or supporting caregivers, she enjoys spending time with her husband, children, and grandchildren, exploring creative outlets, and finding joy in the simple moments of everyday life.

Through this book and her broader mission, LeLe hopes to be a beacon of encouragement, reminding caregivers everywhere that they are not alone—and that their dedication is seen, valued, and profoundly meaningful.

Your Next Step:
Join the B.O.S.S. Caregiver Community!

Caregiving is a journey, but you don't have to walk it alone. You've made it through the pages of this book with courage, reflection, and a heart full of commitment. Now, it's time to turn your insights into action.

Implement the frameworks you've learned. Embrace the B.O.S.S. mindset. Prioritize your own well-being with the same dedication you bring to supporting your loved one. Most importantly, remember that transformation happens best in a community.

Connect, Grow, and Thrive: Connect with a network of like-minded caregivers who understand your challenges, celebrate your victories, and offer practical advice. Whether you need encouragement, expert guidance, or a safe space to be heard, our community supports you.

Ready for Personalized Support?

I'd love to work alongside you if you seek one-on-one coaching to help you balance caregiving, career, and self-care. Together, we'll create a tailored strategy that fits your life—because you deserve support as much as you give it.

Stay Connected: Follow the B.O.S.S. Caregiver Community for daily inspiration and resources:

Instagram: @remedyseniorcare

Facebook: Remedy Senior Care

TikTok: @remedyseniorcare

LinkedIn: Remedy Senior Care

Visit: www.remedyseniorcareconcierge.com/AboutUS

Discover additional caregiving tools, coaching opportunities, and support resources.

Sign Up for Exclusive Resources:

Join my email list for caregiver tips, encouragement, and special offers delivered to your inbox.

www.ingramcontent.com/pod-product-compliance
Lightning Source LLC
Chambersburg PA
CBHW030920140626
46545CB00016B/2335